PRAXIS® 5086 Social Studies: Content and Interpretation

By: Preparing Teachers In America™

This page is intentionally left blank.

This page is intentionally left blank.

Free Online Email Tutoring Services

All preparation guides purchased directly from Preparing Teachers In America includes a free three month email tutoring subscription. Any resale of preparation guides does not qualify for a free email tutoring subscription.

What is Email Tutoring?

Email Tutoring allows buyers to send questions to tutors via email. Buyers can send any questions regarding the exam processes, strategies, content questions, or practice questions.

Preparing Teachers In America reserves the right not to answer questions with or without reason(s).

How to use Email Tutoring?

Buyers need to send an email to onlinepreparationservices@gmail.com requesting email tutoring services. Buyers may be required to confirm the email address used to purchase the preparation guide or additional information prior to using email tutoring. Once email tutoring subscription is confirmed, buyers will be provided an email address to send questions to. The three month period will start the day the subscription is confirmed.

Any misuse of email tutoring services will result in termination of service. Preparing Teachers In America reserves the right to terminate email tutoring subscription at anytime with or without notice.

Comments and Suggestions

All comments and suggestions for improvements for the study guide and email tutoring services need to be sent to onlinepreparationservices@gmail.com.

This page is intentionally left blank.

Table of Content

This page is intentionally left blank.

About the Exam and Study Guide

What is the PRAXIS® 5086 Exam?

The PRAXIS® 5086 is an exam to measure potential teachers' competencies in social studies knowledge. The test measures if individuals have the knowledge necessary to start teaching social studies. The exam is based largely on teacher preparation standards, and the following are content areas covered by the social science exam:

- United States History
- World History
- Government
- Economics
- Geography

The exam is timed at 120 minutes and consists of 90 selected-response questions and three constructed response questions.. The questions are based on knowledge obtained in a bachelor's degree program. The exam contains some questions that may not count toward the score.

What topics are covered on the exam?

The following are some topics covered on the exam:

- historical concepts, terms, sources, and perspective
- development of early civilization
- classical Mediterranean world
- major developments in world history from 500 to 1450
- major developments in early U.S. history
- origins and events of the American Revolution
- causes of the Civil War and Reconstruction
- historical research skills
- impact of major wars in American history
- causes of the Cold War
- the Constitution and the Declaration of Independence

What is included in this study guide book?

This guide includes one full length practice exam for the PRAXIS® 5086 along with detail explanations. The recommendation is to take the exam under exam conditions and a quiet environment.

This page is intentionally left blank.

Practice Test 1

This page is intentionally left blank.

Exam Answer Sheet

Below is an optional answer sheet to use to document answers.

Question Number	Selected Answer	Question Number	Selected Answer	Question Number	Selected Answer
1		31		61	
2		32		62	
3		33		63	
4		34		64	
5		35		65	
6		36		66	
7		37		67	
8		38		68	
9		39		69	
10		40		70	
11		41		71	
12		42		72	
13		43		73	
14		44		74	
15		45		75	
16		46		76	
17		47		77	
18		48		78	
19		49		79	
20		50		80	
21		51		81	
22		52		82	
23		53		83	
24		54		84	
25		55		85	
26		56		86	
27		57		87	
28		58		88	
29		59		89	
30		60		90	

This page is intentionally left blank.

Practice Exam - Questions

QUESTION 1

Which of the following is NOT one of the five pillars of Islam?

- A. reciting the Muslim profession of faith
- B. performing ritual prayers five times each day
- C. giving to the poor
- D. fasting for two months during a year

Answer:

QUESTION 2

Which of the following is the main reason Great Britain established the Proclamation of 1763?

- A. to shun away from the conflicts between American colonists and Native American Indians
- B. to strengthen their economy and to establish more jobs
- C. to acquire additional land west of the Appalachian Mountains
- D. to establish additional laws to ensuring a stable region

Answer:

QUESTION 3

Professor Frederick Jackson Turner was known for the Frontier Thesis. One of the flaws in the Frontier Thesis is that

- A. there was an increase in homesteaders claimed lands after the 1890 Census than before.
- B. the changes that took place in colonial American society when European civilization was transplanted to a wilderness environment.
- C. the increase in population made the assertions in the Frontier Thesis irrelevant.
- D. it lies at the higher end of free land as it is treated as the margin of that settlement which has a density of two or more to the square mile.

Answer:

QUESTION 4

    I.   anticommunism would be the focus of American foreign policy

    II.   opposition to the Sandinista government in Nicaragua

    III.   support for the rebels trying to topple the government in El Salvador

Of the above, which of the following are accurate regarding the Reagan Doctrine?

A. I only
B. I and II
C. I and III
D. II and III

Answer:

QUESTION 5

Vicksburg Campaign was a significant impact to the Civil War because

A. the Confederacy split in two by obtaining control of the Mississippi River.
B. the South controlled portions of the Mississippi River.
C. the campaign caused an increase in population in the South.
D. the Confederacy gain ground and established a strong military base.

Answer:

QUESTION 6

The United States policymakers enacted the Marshall Plan in 1948 mainly

A. to hinder the Soviet Union from gaining advantage of economic distress in Western Europe.
B. to hinder the Soviet Union from gaining land in Western Europe.
C. to promote other nations to establish policies that supported the middle class families.
D. to give aid to Western Europe to rebuild Western European economies.

Answer:

QUESTION 7

The _____ wanted to change the government, social structure, economy, and religion while the _____ sought a change only in government.

    A. French Revolution; War of 1812
    B. Civil War; French Revolution
    C. French Revolution; American Revolution
    D. American Revolution; French Revolution

Answer:

QUESTION 8

Declaration of the Rights of Man and of the Citizen

"The representatives of the French people, . . . believing that the ignorance, neglect, or contempt of the rights of man are the sole cause of public calamities and of the corruption of governments, have determined to set forth in a solemn declaration the natural, unalienable, and sacred rights of man. . .

1. Men are born and remain free and equal in rights. . .

2. The aim of all political association is the preservation of the. . . rights of man. These rights are liberty, property, security and resistance to oppression. . .

5. Law can only prohibit such actions as are hurtful to society. . .

6. Law is the expression of the general will. Every citizen has a right to participate personally, or through his representative, in its formation. It must be the same for all. . .

7. No person shall be accused, arrested, or imprisoned except in the cases and according to the forms prescribed by law. . .

9. As all persons are held innocent until they shall have been declared guilty. . .

11. The free communication of ideas and opinions is one of the most precious of the rights of man. . .

12. A common contribution [tax] is essential. . . This should be equitably distributed among all the citizens in proportion to their means."

The above is an excerpt from the Declaration of the Rights of Man and of the Citizen, which considered which one of the following rights the most precious?

    A. freedom of speech
    B. the right to own slaves
    C. freedom of happiness
    D. freedom of religion

Answer:

QUESTION 9

Pope Gregory IX established the Inquisition in 1231 primarily to

    A. respond to monarchical difficulty.
    B. suppress heretical activities.
    C. establish higher clergy standards across the globe.
    D. establish guidelines for supervising the church across the globe.

Answer:

QUESTION 10

    I.   direct democracy
    II.   obligation to participate
    III.   only adult male citizens debated major issues

The above characteristics best describe which of the following groups in regards to the development of democracy?

    A. modern-American
    B. ancient Athenians
    C. European
    D. Roman Republic

Answer:

QUESTION 11

To protect an infant industry from foreign competitions, the best action is to

    A. shift from an unrestricted international trade to a policy that imposes high tariffs on selected imports.
    B. shift from a restricted international trade to an unrestricted international trade.
    C. shift from a capital market to a market economy market.
    D. lower the price of domestic goods and increase the cost for exports.

Answer:

QUESTION 12

Which of the following was the most significant difficulty for the newly independent African nations after World War II due to the European imperialism?

    A. rebuilding existing infrastructure
    B. existing political boundaries
    C. increasing transportation systems
    D. changing forms of government

Answer:

QUESTION 13

In the sixteenth and seventeenth centuries, new trade routes were opened. What was the major consequence in Europe?

    A. Europeans opened their minds and saw the world in global terms.
    B. Europeans abolished restrictions on trade.
    C. European commercial life shifted to Amsterdam.
    D. European economy was negatively impacted.

Answer:

QUESTION 14

Excerpt from McCulloch v. Maryland (1819)

"If any one proposition could command the universal assent of mankind, we might expect it would be this -- that the Government of the Union, though limited in its powers, is supreme within its sphere of action. This would seem to result necessarily from its nature. It is the Government of all; its powers are delegated by all; it represents all, and acts for all. Though any one State may be willing to control its operations, no State is willing to allow others to control them. The nation, on those subjects on which it can act, must necessarily bind its component parts."

Which of the following subsequent events most strongly reflected the excerpt's view of government?

- A. states nullification of congressional tariff legislation
- B. the victory of the northern unionist in the Civil War
- C. the victory of United States during Spanish-American War
- D. opposition to start the League of Nations

Answer:

QUESTION 15

A change from a direct democracy to a representative democracy is best to undertake when

- A. economic status of people change for the better.
- B. nations acquire additional land.
- C. population increases.
- D. many individuals are not voting.

Answer:

QUESTION 16

Which of the following is the most significant accomplishment of Phoenicians?

A. trade and exploration
B. food
C. technology
D. agriculture

Answer:

QUESTION 17

Which of the following was a major result of Japan's Meiji Restoration?

A. Japan revived some aspects of feudal society.
B. Japan had a culture change.
C. Japan started a modern industrial economy.
D. Japan started to become more open to the world.

Answer:

QUESTION 18

The Native Americans faced a large number of deaths during the colonial period. Of the following, which was the main cause?

A. diseases
B. enslavement
C. water shortage
D. problems due to relocation

Answer:

QUESTION 19

Which of the following best summarizes the minds of most delegates to the Constitutional Convention in 1787 toward the introduction of political parties?

A. Parties would ensure that the delegates would control the government of the new nation.
B. Parties would be beneficial to the growth of democracy.
C. Parties would eventually return the country to dependence on Great Britain.
D. Parties would divide the country and would be disruptive to the conduct of political affairs.

Answer:

QUESTION 20

Which of the following is the primary reason for using literacy tests and poll taxes in many states during Reconstruction?

A. discourage land ownership by African Americans
B. establish new institutions of education for African Americans
C. deprive African Americans of voting rights
D. punish African Americans entrance into the states

Answer:

QUESTION 21

The expansion of Islam between the eighth and twelfth centuries most influenced economic development in the Middle East and Europe through the

A. formation of state agencies that established production standards and set prices for various goods.
B. introduction of crop rotation practices.
C. invention of assembly techniques that increased the productive capacity of contemporary workshops.
D. creation of cities that functioned as centers of commerce and banking.

Answer:

QUESTION 22

After World War II, the United States had a program that provided money, supplies, and machinery to assist European counties in rebuilding. What was the program called?

A. Marshall Plan
B. Four Point Program
C. Truman Doctrine
D. New Deal

Answer:

QUESTION 23

Which of the following is considered primary source(s) in researching the similarities and differences of the Articles of Confederation and the United States Constitution?

I.   the biography of John Hancock
II.   the Bill of Rights
III. John William's personnel account of signing the Articles of Confederation
IV.   interview with historian from the 1800s

A. I and II
B. I and III
C. II and III
D. II and IV

Answer:

QUESTION 24

Which of the following is the best reason for the development of a national market in the United States during the late nineteenth century?

A. expansion of the railroad
B. increase in steel industry
C. initiation of the Interstate Commerce Commission
D. expansion of oil fields

Answer:

QUESTION 25

Which of the following would be considered a primary source for a research project about the World War II?

    A. an encyclopedia article
    B. a letter written by a soldier to his brother during the war
    C. a biography of a prominent Union general during the war
    D. a novel set in northern Virginia that takes place during the war

Answer:

QUESTION 26

Japan invaded India during World War II mainly because India

    A. was controlled by Japan's enemies.
    B. had once attacked Japan.
    C. had many natural resources.
    D. was a strategic location.

Answer:

QUESTION 27

The political situation in Africa today is heartening and at the same time disturbing. It is heartening to see so many new flags hoisted in place of the old; it is disturbing to see so many countries of varying sizes and at different levels of development, weak and, in some cases, almost helpless…The greatest contribution that Africa can make to the peace of the world is to avoid all the dangers inherent in disunity, by creating a political union which will also by its success, stand as an example to a divided world…The scant attention paid to African opposition to the French atomic tests in the Sahara, and the ignominious spectacle of the U.N. in the Congo quibbling about constitutional niceties while the Republic was tottering into anarchy, are evidence of the callous disregard of African Independence by the Great Powers. We have to prove that greatness is not to be measured in stockpiles of atom bombs.

The above is excerpt from Kwame Nkrumah, first President of Ghana. His ideas in the passage above are most representative of the ideology of

    A. liberation theology movement.
    B. anti-apartheid movement.
    C. Pan-Africanism.
    D. African American.

Answer:

QUESTION 28

While conducting research on the United States politics of the late nineteenth century, a historian considers consulting the autobiography of a prominent politician who was alive in the late nineteenth century. Doing so is most likely to help the historian

    A. evaluate the long-term consequences of decisions made in the late nineteenth century.
    B. determine the exact sequence of events.
    C. obtain insight into contemporary values and beliefs.
    D. give perspective of individuals' feeling in the late nineteenth century.

Answer:

QUESTION 29

Andrew Jackson's spoil system favored which group of individuals?

   A. merchant
   B. political advocates
   C. peasants
   D. common people

Answer:

QUESTION 30

House Democrats overwhelmingly oppose the agreement, largely because of concerns of labor unions that the agreement would not adequately protect the rights of low-paid workers in Central America who would be competing more directly with U.S. workers. Many pro-trade, centrist Democrats are also declaring their opposition in order to voice their broader disagreement with Bush administration tax and domestic spending policies that they argue are not doing enough to equip the workforce to deal with a changing global economy.

The leaders of the Republican opposition to CAFTA are Reps. Walter B. Jones Jr. (N.C.) and Virgil H. Goode Jr. (Va.), both former Democrats. A number of Republicans who represent once-Democratic southern congressional districts heavily dependent on agricultural subsidies and tariff and quota protections for textiles also object to the treaty.

Under CAFTA, the United States would make permanent the temporary suspension of tariffs set by the Caribbean Basin Initiative. In return, the Dominican Republic, Honduras, Costa Rica, El Salvador, Guatemala and Nicaragua would reduce or eliminate tariffs on most imports, open state monopolies to foreign competition, and remove legal barriers to foreign investment.

Brown and Jones predicted the administration will begin offering special favors to wavering lawmakers. "They are going to open the bank for these guys," said Brown, citing past offers of bridges and other public works projects to win votes on controversial trade bills.

Washington Post, June 12, 2005

Based on the above reading from the Washington Post, the method likely to be effective for the White House to implement in passing the free trade legislation is

    A. executive order
    B. media
    C. pocket veto
    D. logrolling

Answer:

QUESTION 31

> No one should be disquieted on account of his opinions, including his religious views, provided their manifestation does not disturb the public order established by law. - **French Declaration of the Rights of Man and Citizen (1789)**

The ideas and principles expressed in the quote above are most closely related to which of the following Enlightenment philosophers?

A. Voltaire
B. Jean-Jacques Rousseau
C. Baron de Montesquieu
D. Denis Diderot

Answer:

QUESTION 32

Which of the following appropriately describes a major check on the United States Supreme Court's power?

A. The Court has no authority in enforcing decisions.
B. The Court has no authority to modifying decisions.
C. The Court has no authority to overturning executive orders.
D. The Court can only hear cases that went through lower courts.

Answer:

QUESTION 33

    I.   clearer separation of power between the branches of government

    II.   roles and responsibilities of public officials clearly outlined

    III.   greater cooperation between branches of government

Of the above, which of the following describes difference/differences between parliamentary democracies such as Great Britain and presidential democracies such as the United States?

    A. I only
    B. I and II
    C. I and III
    D. I, II and II

Answer:

QUESTION 34

> In all criminal prosecutions, the accused shall enjoy the right to a speedy and public trial, by an impartial jury of the state and district wherein the crime shall have been committed, which district shall have been previously ascertained by law, and to be informed of the nature and cause of the accusation; to be confronted with the witnesses against him; . . . and to have the assistance of counsel for his defense. – United States Constitution

In the quote from the United States Constitution, the meaning of which of the terms is best articulated?

    A. jurisdiction
    B. due process requirements
    C. equal protection
    D. witness protection

Answer:

QUESTION 35

Which of the following events is most credited for surfacing the concept of natural rights?

A. Enlightenment Period
B. Industrial Revolution
C. Age of Exploration
D. Civil War

Answer:

QUESTION 36

1. Bill is referred to appropriate committee
2. Names
3. Voted on
4. Signed by the president

The above process best reflects which of the following?

A. pass a bill into a law in the House of Representatives
B. pass a bill into a law in the Senate
C. pass a bill into law under emergency conditions
D. pass a bill into law in Congress

Answer:

QUESTION 37

In the late nineteenth-century, America saw the expansion of the railroad system and the most significant result was

A. increase jobs.
B. spread of ideas.
C. exchange of goods.
D. more focus on technology.

Answer:

QUESTION 38

Which of the following constitutional provisions reflect the increasing intersectional tension within United States during 1850s?

    A. "No preference shall be given by any regulation of commerce or revenue to the ports of one state over those of another."
    B. "The President shall be Commander in Chief of the army and navy of the United States, and of the militia of the several states, when called into the actual service of the United States."
    C. "No state shall enter into any treaty, alliance, or confederation; grant letters of marque or reprisal; coin money; [or] emit bills of credit."
    D. "The Congress shall have power to dispose of and make all needful rules and regulations respecting the territory or other property belonging to the United States."

Answer:

QUESTION 39

Which of the following source is not useful in obtaining information about the Presidency of Richard Nixon?

    A. Richard Nixon's autobiography
    B. Speeches of Richard Nixon
    C. White House correspondence
    D. Richard Nixon's resignation letter

Answer:

QUESTION 40

The major reason for the extraordinary economic affluence of United States society approximately twenty years after World War II was because of which of the following?

    A. the United States industrial base was undamaged
    B. no major competition in the global market
    C. the devolution of the United States to become a superpower
    D. increase in wage control and exports and imports

Answer:

QUESTION 41

Bill of Rights is the first ten amendments to the United States Constitution. Which of the following principles of the United States Constitution best demonstrate the idea of the Bill of Rights?

    A. ability to overthrow government
    B. limited government
    C. rights of the people
    D. checks and balances

Answer:

QUESTION 42

Which of the following geographic factors had the most significant influence on economic life in the early life of the people of Anatolia?

    A. the natural harbors along the Red Sea
    B. the aquatic resources of the Mediterranean Sea
    C. the resources of the Eastern Desert
    D. the annual flooding of the Nile River

Answer:

QUESTION 43

A recent college graduate is debating whether he should continue to obtain his graduate degree or accept a job offer for entry level position. Which of the economic concepts applies most directly to the decision the graduate is attempting to make?

    A. supply and demand
    B. cost of opportunity
    C. market demand
    D. productivity

Answer:

QUESTION 44

The Declaration of Independence states, "That whenever any form of government becomes destructive of these ends, it is the Right of the People to alter or abolish it." This statement describe the enlightened idea of a

    A. strong democracy.
    B. return to a society that has two central authority.
    C. social contract between the government and the people.
    D. right to overthrow the current government.

Answer:

QUESTION 45

The following changes occurred in the United States in the 19th Century:

    • improvements in agricultural production
    • increases in immigration from Europe
    • advancements in networks of railroad

The changes resulted in:

    A. removal of large suburbs around cities
    B. growth of urban areas
    C. obtaining overseas territories
    D. movement of people from the urban to rural areas

Answer:

QUESTION 46

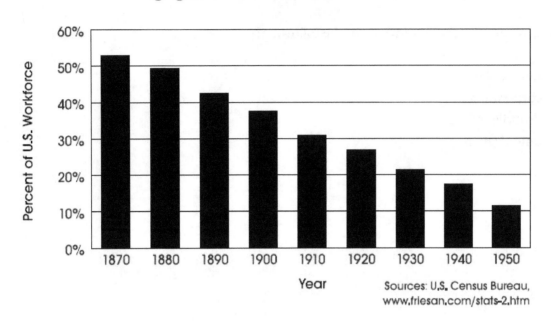

Percent of U.S. Workforce Engaged in Farm Labor, 1870 – 1950

Sources: U.S. Census Bureau,
www.friesan.com/stats-2.htm

According to the graph above, the trend shown in the graph is associated with?

A. decreased immigration
B. increased urbanization
C. reduced population growth
D. advances in communication

Answer:

QUESTION 47

I.   ability to sell stocks
II.   limited liability for owners
III. improved ability to raise large sums of money

The items above are all benefits of which of the following?

A.   monopolies
B.   corporations
C.   proprietorships
D.   unionization

Answer:

QUESTION 48

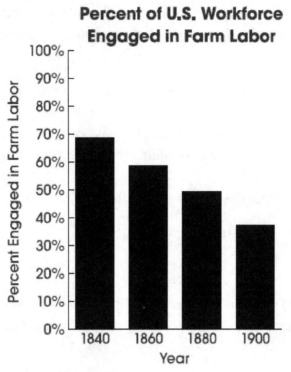

In the above graph, what effect of 19th century industrialization in the United States is shown in the above graph?

A. emigration from the United States
B. increased regulation of child labor
C. decreased demand for farm products
D. modernization of agriculture

Answer:

QUESTION 49

The scientific revolution of the sixteenth and seventeenth centuries contributed most significantly in the thoughts fostered during the Enlightenment Period by which of the following?

    A. The use of math to assist in understanding the relationships among diverse natural events.
    B. The use of reason to devise laws to explain the physical world.
    C. The use of science to assist in understanding the relationships among diverse natural events.
    D. The use of math to devise the laws to explain the physical world.

Answer:

QUESTION 50

Steam power was a critical invention in American History. During the earlier part of the nineteenth century, the increase usage of stem power directly resulted in all the following except?

    A. revenue of factories
    B. location of factories
    C. productivity of factor
    D. quality of goods produced

Answer:

QUESTION 51

In the late nineteenth century and early twentieth century, as a result of industrialization, progressive reformers wanted government regulation of business in order to

    A. stop companies from moving their factories to other countries.
    B. return competition by limiting the power of monopolies.
    C. control inflation and recession.
    D. provide money for public services.

Answer:

QUESTION 52

When a country's constitution mandates the branches of government to remain independent of other branches, it is adhering to the constitutional principle of

    A. checks and balances.
    B. separation of powers.
    C. popular sovereignty.
    D. bipartisanism.

Answer:

QUESTION 53

The United States Declaration of Independence and the French Declaration of the Rights of Man share the similarity by expressing the idea that governments must

    A. provide equal rights to all men.
    B. protect the right of people.
    C. support religious beliefs.
    D. provide equal education all individuals.

Answer:

QUESTION 54

In Southern states, sharecropping became a significant means of organizing agricultural production due to

    A. signing of the Emancipation Proclamation.
    B. the need to generate cash in the short term.
    C. the refusal of Northern financiers to extend loans.
    D. the long-term effect of Civil War.

Answer:

QUESTION 55

Which of the following is NOT a difference between the northern and southern sections of the United States between 1800 and 1860 prior to the Civil War?

    A. Larger population of European immigrants who settled in the northern states, resulting in greater population growth in the North as oppose to the South.
    B. The North had much more industrialized economy than the South.
    C. During the first half of the nineteenth century, factory production played an important role in the southern economy while agricultural played an important role in the northern economy.
    D. After the American Revolution, northern states gradually abolished slavery while human bondage remained a central feature of southern society.

Answer:

QUESTION 56

Which of the following is NOT an important relationship between the civil rights movement and the Civil War?

    A. Many African Americans and whites united to protest the racism and discrimination that existed in the United States.
    B. A more organized Civil Rights Movement came into being.
    C. During the 1950s and the early 1960s, Martin Luther King, Jr., emerged as an important leader of the Civil Rights Movement.
    D. Economic competition with the Soviet Union resulted in greater injustice in the United States among whites and blacks.

Answer:

QUESTION 57

Following World War II, the economic recovery of Japan primarily focused on

    A. developing an export economy.
    B. developing an import economy.
    C. rebuilding strong military.
    D. developing an agricultural economy.

Answer:

QUESTION 58

In Latin American, all the following have limited development of transportation systems and communication system except?

    A. deserts
    B. rain forests
    C. river systems
    D. mountain regions

Answer:

QUESTION 59

    I.   First Gulf War – President George H.W. Bush

    II.   World War I – President Woodrow Wilson

    III.   Vietnam War – President Gerald Ford

Of the above, which of the following accurately indicate the President during the war?

    A. I, II, and III

    B. I only

    C. II only

    D. I and II

Answer:

QUESTION 60

Increase use of renewable fuels such as solar power or wind power could result in

    A. increase use of coal.

    B. increase dependence on nuclear generated power.

    C. less pollution in the environment.

    D. needing more foreign oil.

Answer:

QUESTION 61

How do people survive in harsh environments such as the desert?

    A. They relocate to a better location.
    B. They adapt and make changes to their environment.
    C. They find food and shelter to meets needs.
    D. They establish civilization.

Answer:

QUESTION 62

Which of the following was a main cause of the Cold War between the United States and the Soviet Union?

    A. desire to have greater influence on world economy
    B. desire to have greater influence on other nations
    C. desire to have greater control over oil prices
    D. desire to have greater control over export laws

Answer:

QUESTION 63

> One way of life is based upon the will of the people, and is distinguished by ... freedom from political oppression. The second way of life is based on the will of a minority forcibly imposed upon the will of the majority. It relies upon ...the suppression of personal freedoms.

In 1947, the above quote was delivered as part of which of the following speech?

    A. Monroe Doctrine
    B. Truman Doctrine
    C. New Deal Speech
    D. New Frontier

Answer:

QUESTION 64

Which of the following is NOT a depiction of Hitler's Germany, Mussolini's Italy, and Stalin's Russia?

A. All nations were totalitarian governments.
B. Economy was governed by Marxist principles.
C. Political opponents were tortured in each state.
D. Desired to expand their borders.

Answer:

QUESTION 65

Which of the following was impacted the most due to the distribution of hydrocarbon resources in Africa, Latin America, and Middle East during the 20th century?

A. United States economy
B. world economy
C. international relations
D. price of oil

Answer:

QUESTION 66

In developed countries, around year 2000, majority of the people resided in towns and cities. Two hundred years prior, the population resided in rural areas. Which of the following most significantly contributed to the change?

A. increase in birth
B. modernization of transportation
C. industrialization of national economies
D. increase infrastructure

Answer:

QUESTION 67

What is a major difference between Buddhism and Hinduism?

A. Buddhism refused the need for caste and rite to achieve nirvana.
B. Buddhism was polytheistic and Hinduism was monotheistic.
C. Buddhism did not accept the political world
D. Hinduism focused on respect and not hurting individuals

Answer:

QUESTION 68

I.   rulers functioned as religious leader as well as heads of state
II. a class system based on merits and values
III. a military based on only volunteer service

Of the above, which is/are common characteristic(s) of both Aztec and Incan civilizations?

A. I only
B. III only
C. I and II
D. II and III

Answer:

QUESTION 69

Leaders of the Chinese Revolution broke most determinedly with Chinese past in their

A. emphasizes on materialism, science, and class conflict.
B. refusal to engage in other nations.
C. creation of a centralized government.
D. principal of communism.

Answer:

QUESTION 70

Which of the following is incorrectly defined?

	Type of Society	Definition
A	Hunting and Gathering Societies	Those peoples whose technology is de-signed to use primarily wild game and plant resources.
B	Horticultural Societies	People who depend the raising of livestock.
C	Agrarian Societies	Societies that depend mainly on plant cultivation, and that use draft animals and plows.
D	Commercial/Industrial Societies	Societies with a majority of the population engaged in trade and manufacturing.

Answer:

QUESTION 71

Compared to river valley culture in Egypt and Mesopotamia, Chinese civilization

  A. had no reliable artifact left behind to study the civilization.
  B. probably did not rely on irrigation as other civilization did.
  C. likely developed after the Mesopotamia and Nile Valley civilization.
  D. likely developed at the same time as Mesopotamia and Nile Valley civilization.

Answer:

QUESTION 72

How did the Constitution address the quote: "He [King George III] has affected to render the Military independent of and superior to Civil power…?"

  A. the Constitution states that the president is the commander-in-chief of the military
  B. the Constitution prevents any revisions unless authorized by the president
  C. provided voting rights to all Americans
  D. gave citizens the right to bear arms

Answer:

QUESTION 73

All the following are features of the Sumerian civilization except?

    A. an alphabet of 22 letters
    B. city-states
    C. ziggurats
    D. cuneiform

Answer:

QUESTION 74

Which of the following is the best way a president can influence the opinions of the federal judiciary?

    A. increasing the number of justices on Supreme Court
    B. replacing Supreme Court justices at the beginning of the term
    C. appointing justices who share common political views
    D. keeping a personal relationship with the justices

Answer:

QUESTION 75

Which line on the table best matches a historical research question with the source of information that can used in providing information?

Line	Research Question	Source of Information
1	How did World War II impact the United States in the long term?	historical atlas
2	What roots did the principles of the Bill of Rights express?	biographical dictionary
3	How has the proportion of China population living in rural areas changed in the past decade?	almanac
4	How is the safety of our school system compared to several decades ago?	encyclopedia

    A. Line 1
    B. Line 2
    C. Line 3
    D. Line 4

Answer:

QUESTION 76

A librarian is doing a lesson on effective ways of teaching for group of middle school students. The topic for the week is primary and secondary sources. Librarian can inform the students that the most effective way to identify relevant secondary and primary sources is by

A. asking the teacher prior to making any conclusions.
B. consulting online research for confirmation purposes.
C. reviewing the citations and bibliography of texts related to the topics of research.
D. seeing what year the source was written and decide if it primary or secondary.

Answer:

QUESTION 77

A nation large in size with a heterogeneous population and conflicting needs is best suited with which type of government system?

A. unitary system
B. communistic system
C. federal system
D. state system

Answer:

QUESTION 78

I.   Department of Education
II.   Securities and Exchange Commission
III.   Environmental Protection Agency

Of the above, which of the following policymaking powers is/are based on delegated legislative authority?

A. I only
B. I and II
C. I and III
D. II and III

Answer:

QUESTION 79

	Building Art Exhibit		Expanding Library	
	Yes	No	Yes	No
James County	22,323	20,329	18,929	21,932

James County is looking to build an art exhibit or expand the library with tax payer funds. The above results were obtained in a recent special election on the issue. A history teacher wants to determine whether the residents of the country held strong opinions about these two issues. Clearly, the results above will support the researcher in the study, but what additional information will be most useful to the teacher?

    A. the age group of the individuals who voted
    B. any voters who would be bias in voting
    C. number of individuals who were eligible to vote
    D. the cost of building the exhibit and expanding the library

Answer:

QUESTION 80

Which of the following is NOT an enumerated power of Congress?

    A. declare war
    B. treaty ratification
    C. establish post offices
    D. all the above are powers of Congress

Answer:

QUESTION 81

Which of the following powers allows Congress to indirectly impact foreign policy?

    A. approve and reject treaties
    B. approve or reject presidential appointments
    C. allocate federal funding
    D. regulate international commerce

Answer:

QUESTION 82

Social status is more likely to be determined by values not related to money in a pre-industrial society as oppose to which of the following society?

    A. industrial
    B. post industrial
    C. post Civil War
    D. post World War II

Answer:

QUESTION 83

    I.   weakened the economics of major colonial power
    II.   increased prewar alliances major powers
    III. demolished prewar alliances major powers

Which of the above is way(s) did World War II impacted the decolonization in Africa and Asia?

    A. I only
    B. II only
    C. III only
    D. I and II

Answer:

QUESTION 84

Who was the first woman to contribute to women's right to vote?

    A. Eleanor Roosevelt
    B. Susan B. Anthony
    C. Elizabeth Cady Stanton
    D. Rosa Parks

Answer:

QUESTION 85

    I.   granting titles of nobility
    II.   coining money
    III.   establishing qualifications for voting

Under the Constitution, which is/are allowed to be undertaken by the states?

    A. I only
    B. III only
    C. I and II
    D. I and III

Answer:

QUESTION 86

Level of Education	Average Salary
Doctoral Degree	$90,000
Master's Degree	$70,000
Bachelor's Degree	$60,000
Associate Degree	$50,000
Some College	$40,000
High School Graduate	$30,000
Some High School	$20,000

Which of the following conclusion can be made from the table?

A. A doctoral degree will always make more than other degrees.
B. Level of education is proportionally related to salary.
C. Level of education is not proportionally related to salary.
D. The quality of life for high school student is not going to be good as a college student.

Answer:

QUESTION 87

Which of the following is true about the Federal Reserve System?

A. its seven Board members are appointed by the President of the United States
B. its main policy-making body is called the CBO
C. it insures checking accounts against bank failure
D. it accepts deposits from individuals and makes loans for mortgages

Answer:

QUESTION 88

    I.   decreased domestic investments
    II.   increased private saving
   III. decreased foreign investments

Of the above, which is/are way(s) to finance a budget deficit?

    A. I only
    B. III only
    C. I and II
    D. I, II, and III

Answer:

QUESTION 89

John has a large sum of money to invest. He is very concerned with the risk, but not with the a large return. What is the best investment for him?

    A. checking account
    B. saving account
    C. real estate
    D. stock market

Answer:

QUESTION 90

Which of the following is simple economic model illustrating the flow of goods and services?

    A. Circular flow model
    B. Loanable fund model
    C. Static model
    D. Dynamic model

Answer:

Constructed Response Questions

Question 1

Read the information below; then complete the exercise that follows.

In American history, many significant documents have been written that has shaped our society today.

Bill of Rights, Declaration of Independence, Articles of Confederation, Common Sense

Using your knowledge of U.S. history, select two of the above documents and in your response:

- discuss two similarities of the documents
- discuss two differences of the documents
- discuss the long term impact of the documents

Question 2

Read the two passages below; then complete the exercise that follows.

Alexander Hamilton, The Report on Manufactures (December 5, 1791)
The expediency of encouraging manufactures in the United States appears at this time to be pretty generally admitted. Not only the wealth, but the independence and security of a country, appear to be materially connected with the prosperity of manufactures. Every nation, with a view to those great objects, ought to endeavor to possess within itself all the essentials of national supply. These comprise the means of subsistence, habitation, clothing, and defense. A full view having now been taken of the inducements to the promotion of manufactures in the United States, it is proper to consider the means by which it may be effected. In countries where there is great private wealth, much may be effected by the voluntary contributions of patriotic individuals; but in a community situated like that of the United States, the public purse must apply the deficiency of private resource. In what can it be so useful, as in prompting and improving the efforts of industry?

Thomas Jefferson, Notes on the State of Virginia (1784)
Those who labour in the earth are the chosen people of God, if ever he had a chosen people, whose breasts he has made his peculiar deposit for substantial and genuine virtue. Corruption of morals in the mass of cultivators is a phenomenon of which no age nor nation has furnished an example. It is the mark set on those, who not looking up to heaven, to their own soil and industry, as does the husbandman, for their subsistence, depend for it [instead] on the casualties and caprice of customers. Dependence begets subservience and venality, suffocates the germ of virtue, and prepares fit tools for the designs of ambition. [G]enerally speaking, the proportion which the aggregate of the other classes of citizens bears in any state to that of its husbandmen, is the proportion of its unsound to its healthy parts, and is a good-enough barometer whereby to measure its degree of corruption. While we have land to labour then, let us never wish to see our citizens occupied at a work-bench, or twirling a distaff.

Using your knowledge of U.S. history, prepare a narrative response in which you:

- explain the background historical context on how the two documents surfaced
- compare and contrast the governmental actions Jefferson and Hamilton would likely support based on the excerpts

Question 3

Analyze why some United States economists support and other United States economists resist on the idea of removing all restraints on the flow of capital and goods.

This page is intentionally left blank.

Practice Exam - Correct Answer Sheet

Below is an optional answer sheet to use to document answers.

Question Number	Correct Answer	Question Number	Correct Answer	Question Number	Correct Answer
1	D	31	A	61	B
2	A	32	A	62	B
3	A	33	A	63	B
4	B	34	B	64	B
5	A	35	A	65	C
6	A	36	A	66	C
7	C	37	C	67	A
8	A	38	D	68	A
9	B	39	A	69	A
10	B	40	B	70	B
11	A	41	B	71	C
12	B	42	B	72	D
13	A	43	B	73	A
14	B	44	C	74	C
15	C	45	B	75	C
16	A	46	B	76	C
17	C	47	B	77	C
18	A	48	D	78	D
19	D	49	B	79	C
20	C	50	D	80	D
21	D	51	B	81	C
22	A	52	B	82	B
23	C	53	B	83	A
24	A	54	D	84	C
25	B	55	C	85	B
26	A	56	D	86	B
27	C	57	A	87	A
28	C	58	A	88	D
29	D	59	A	89	B
30	D	60	C	90	A

NOTE: Getting approximately 80% of the questions correct increases chances of obtaining passing score on the real exam. This varies from different states and university programs.

This page is intentionally left blank.

Practice Exam - Questions and Explanations

QUESTION 1

Which of the following is NOT one of the five pillars of Islam?

- A. reciting the Muslim profession of faith
- B. performing ritual prayers five times each day
- C. giving to the poor
- D. fasting for two months during a year

Answer: D

Explanation: Fasting is required in Islam, but not for two months during a year. Fasting is only required for one month, which is the month of Ramadan.

QUESTION 2

Which of the following is the main reason Great Britain established the Proclamation of 1763?

- A. to shun away from the conflicts between American colonists and Native American Indians
- B. to strengthen their economy and to establish more jobs
- C. to acquire additional land west of the Appalachian Mountains
- D. to establish additional laws to ensuring a stable region

Answer: A

Explanation: The Proclamation of 1763 was issued by King George III following Great Britain's acquisition of French territory in North America after the end of the French and Indian War. The Proclamation was to shun away from the conflicts between American colonists and Native American Indians.

QUESTION 3

Professor Frederick Jackson Turner was known for the Frontier Thesis. One of the flaws in the Frontier Thesis is that

A. there was an increase in homesteaders claimed lands after the 1890 Census than before.
B. the changes that took place in colonial American society when European civilization was transplanted to a wilderness environment.
C. the increase in population made the assertions in the Frontier Thesis irrelevant.
D. it lies at the higher end of free land as it is treated as the margin of that settlement which has a density of two or more to the square mile.

Answer: A

Explanation: One of the flaws in the Frontier Thesis is that there was an increase in homesteaders claimed lands after the 1890 Census than before.

QUESTION 4

I.   anticommunism would be the focus of American foreign policy
II.   opposition to the Sandinista government in Nicaragua
III.   support for the rebels trying to topple the government in El Salvador

Of the above, which of the following are accurate regarding the Reagan Doctrine?

A. I only
B. I and II
C. I and III
D. II and III

Answer: B

Explanation: The Reagan Doctrine emphasized that anticommunism would be the focus of American foreign policy. The Reagan Doctrine also refers to the opposition to the Sandinista government in Nicaragua.

QUESTION 5

Vicksburg Campaign was a significant impact to the Civil War because

- A. the Confederacy split in two by obtaining control of the Mississippi River.
- B. the South controlled portions of the Mississippi River.
- C. the campaign caused an increase in population in the South.
- D. the Confederacy gain ground and established a strong military base.

Answer: A

Explanation: The Vicksburg Campaign was a series of battles in the Western Theater of the American Civil War directed against Vicksburg, Mississippi. Vicksburg Campaign was a significant impact to the Civil War because the Confederacy split in two by obtaining control of the Mississippi River.

QUESTION 6

The United States policymakers enacted the Marshall Plan in 1948 mainly

- A. to hinder the Soviet Union from gaining advantage of economic distress in Western Europe.
- B. to hinder the Soviet Union from gaining land in Western Europe.
- C. to promote other nations to establish policies that supported the middle class families.
- D. to give aid to Western Europe to rebuild Western European economies.

Answer: A

Explanation: The Marshall Plan of 1948 was to give aid to Western Europe to rebuild Western European economies, but the main reason for the Marshall Plan in 1948 was to hinder the Soviet Union from gaining advantage of economic distress in Western Europe.

QUESTION 7

The _____ wanted to change the government, social structure, economy, and religion while the _____ sought a change only in government.

    A. French Revolution; War of 1812
    B. Civil War; French Revolution
    C. French Revolution; American Revolution
    D. American Revolution; French Revolution

Answer: C

Explanation: The French Revolution wanted to change the government, social structure, economy, and religion while the American Revolution sought a change only in government.

QUESTION 8

Declaration of the Rights of Man and of the Citizen

"The representatives of the French people, . . . believing that the ignorance, neglect, or contempt of the rights of man are the sole cause of public calamities and of the corruption of governments, have determined to set forth in a solemn declaration the natural, unalienable, and sacred rights of man. . .

1. Men are born and remain free and equal in rights. . .

2. The aim of all political association is the preservation of the. . . rights of man. These rights are liberty, property, security and resistance to oppression. . .

5. Law can only prohibit such actions as are hurtful to society. . .

6. Law is the expression of the general will. Every citizen has a right to participate personally, or through his representative, in its formation. It must be the same for all. . .

7. No person shall be accused, arrested, or imprisoned except in the cases and according to the forms prescribed by law. . .

9. As all persons are held innocent until they shall have been declared guilty. . .

11. The free communication of ideas and opinions is one of the most precious of the rights of man. . .

12. A common contribution [tax] is essential. . . This should be equitably distributed among all the citizens in proportion to their means."

The above is an excerpt from the Declaration of the Rights of Man and of the Citizen, which considered which one of the following rights the most precious?

    A. freedom of speech
    B. the right to own slaves
    C. freedom of happiness
    D. freedom of religion

Answer: A

Explanation: One of the most precious rights of the Declaration of the Rights of Man and of the Citizen is freedom of speech.

QUESTION 9

Pope Gregory IX established the Inquisition in 1231 primarily to

- A. respond to monarchical difficulty.
- B. suppress heretical activities.
- C. establish higher clergy standards across the globe.
- D. establish guidelines for supervising the church across the globe.

Answer: B

Explanation: Pope Gregory IX established the Inquisition in 1231 primarily to suppress heretical activities.

QUESTION 10

I.	direct democracy
II.	obligation to participate
III.	only adult male citizens debated major issues

The above characteristics best describe which of the following groups in regards to the development of democracy?

- A. modern-American
- B. ancient Athenians
- C. European
- D. Roman Republic

Answer: B

Explanation: Direct democracy, obligation to participate, and all adult male citizens' debated major issues are characteristics that best describe the democracy of ancient Athenians.

QUESTION 11

To protect an infant industry from foreign competitions, the best action is to

- A. shift from an unrestricted international trade to a policy that imposes high tariffs on selected imports.
- B. shift from a restricted international trade to an unrestricted international trade.
- C. shift from a capital market to a market economy market.
- D. lower the price of domestic goods and increase the cost for exports.

Answer: A

Explanation: To protect an infant industry from foreign competition, the best action is to shift from an unrestricted international trade to a policy that imposes high tariffs on selected imports. Foreign competitions will be negatively impacted with additional high tariffs on selected imports.

QUESTION 12

Which of the following was the most significant difficulty for the newly independent African nations after World War II due to the European imperialism?

- A. rebuilding existing infrastructure
- B. existing political boundaries
- C. increasing transportation systems
- D. changing forms of government

Answer: B

Explanation: Newly independent African nations had difficulty with existing political boundaries after World War II due to the European imperialism.

QUESTION 13

In the sixteenth and seventeenth centuries, new trade routes were opened. What was the major consequence in Europe?

    A. Europeans opened their minds and saw the world in global terms.
    B. Europeans abolished restrictions on trade.
    C. European commercial life shifted to Amsterdam.
    D. European economy was negatively impacted.

Answer: A

Explanation: Trade allowed the exchange of spices, silks, and other commodities, which were rare in Europe. With the exchange of goods and new trade routes, there were also ideas entering into Europe. Overall, Europeans opened their minds and saw the world in global terms.

QUESTION 14

Excerpt from McCulloch v. Maryland (1819)

"If any one proposition could command the universal assent of mankind, we might expect it would be this -- that the Government of the Union, though limited in its powers, is supreme within its sphere of action. This would seem to result necessarily from its nature. It is the Government of all; its powers are delegated by all; it represents all, and acts for all. Though any one State may be willing to control its operations, no State is willing to allow others to control them. The nation, on those subjects on which it can act, must necessarily bind its component parts."

Which of the following subsequent events most strongly reflected the excerpt's view of government?

    A. states nullification of congressional tariff legislation
    B. the victory of the northern unionist in the Civil War
    C. the victory of United States during Spanish-American War
    D. opposition to start the League of Nations

Answer: B

Explanation: The victory of the northern unionist in the Civil War reflects the excerpt. The Civil War was regarding control, which reflects the statement "any one State may be willing to control its operations, no State is willing to allow others to control them".

QUESTION 15

A change from a direct democracy to a representative democracy is best to undertake when

    A. economic status of people change for the better.
    B. nations acquire additional land.
    C. population increases.
    D. many individuals are not voting.

Answer: C

Explanation: Representative democracy is when elected individuals represent a group of individuals in the democratic process. Direct democracy is when the people directly decide. Representative democracy is best when there is an increase in population as process is simplified.

QUESTION 16

Which of the following is the most significant accomplishment of Phoenicians?

    A. trade and exploration
    B. food
    C. technology
    D. agriculture

Answer: A

Explanation: Phoenicia was an ancient civilization consisting of independent city-state along the coast of the Mediterranean Sea. One of the most significant accomplishments of Phoenicians was trade and exploration.

QUESTION 17

Which of the following was a major result of Japan's Meiji Restoration?

    A. Japan revived some aspects of feudal society.
    B. Japan had a culture change.
    C. Japan started a modern industrial economy.
    D. Japan started to become more open to the world.

Answer: C

Explanation: Meiji Restoration was the political revolution of 1868 that brought the end of Tokugawa military government. The control was returned to direct imperial rule under Mutsuhito. After that, there was a significant change in politics and economy. In particular, Japan started a modern industrial economy with development of strategic industries, transportation, and communications.

QUESTION 18

The Native Americans faced a large number of deaths during the colonial period. Of the following, which was the main cause?

    A. diseases
    B. enslavement
    C. water shortage
    D. problems due to relocation

Answer: A

Explanation: Diseases caused a large number of Native Americans deaths during the colonial period.

QUESTION 19

Which of the following best summarizes the minds of most delegates to the Constitutional Convention in 1787 toward the introduction of political parties?

    A. Parties would ensure that the delegates would control the government of the new nation.
    B. Parties would be beneficial to the growth of democracy.
    C. Parties would eventually return the country to dependence on Great Britain.
    D. Parties would divide the country and would be disruptive to the conduct of political affairs.

Answer: D

Explanation: In 1787, delegates to the Constitutional Convention feared that parties would divide the country and would be disruptive to the conduct of political affairs.

QUESTION 20

Which of the following is the primary reason for using literacy tests and poll taxes in many states during Reconstruction?

    A. discourage land ownership by African Americans
    B. establish new institutions of education for African Americans
    C. deprive African Americans of voting rights
    D. punish African Americans entrance into the states

Answer: C

Explanation: After African Americans obtain the right to vote, individuals continued to prevent African Americans to vote. This was done by implementing policies that required literacy tests and poll taxes, knowing that this would lower African Americans participation in voting.

QUESTION 21

The expansion of Islam between the eighth and twelfth centuries most influenced economic development in the Middle East and Europe through the

- A. formation of state agencies that established production standards and set prices for various goods.
- B. introduction of crop rotation practices.
- C. invention of assembly techniques that increased the productive capacity of contemporary workshops.
- D. creation of cities that functioned as centers of commerce and banking.

Answer: D

Explanation: The expansion of Islam between the eighth and twelfth centuries most influenced economic development in the Middle East and Europe through the establishment of cities that functioned as centers of commerce and banking.

QUESTION 22

After World War II, the United States had a program that provided money, supplies, and machinery to assist European counties in rebuilding. What was the program called?

- A. Marshall Plan
- B. Four Point Program
- C. Truman Doctrine
- D. New Deal

Answer: A

Explanation: The Marshall Plan was an American initiative to aid billions of dollars to Western Europe to rebuild Western European economies after World War II.

QUESTION 23

Which of the following is considered primary source(s) in researching the similarities and differences of the Articles of Confederation and the United States Constitution?

    I.   the biography of John Hancock
    II.   the Bill of Rights
    III.   John William's personnel account of signing the Articles of Confederation
    IV.   interview with historian from the 1800s

  A. I and II
  B. I and III
  C. II and III
  D. II and IV

Answer: C

Explanation: The Bill of Rights and John William's personnel account of signing the Articles of Confederation were written during the time of the development of the Articles of Confederation and the United States Constitution.

QUESTION 24

Which of the following is the best reason for the development of a national market in the United States during the late nineteenth century?

  A. expansion of the railroad
  B. increase in steel industry
  C. initiation of the Interstate Commerce Commission
  D. expansion of oil fields

Answer: A

Explanation: The early American economy had smaller, local markets centered in or around big cities. With the expansion of the railroad, the goods could be reached in other regions. In other words, the country was more connected together in a national market.

QUESTION 25

Which of the following would be considered a primary source for a research project about the World War II?

  A. an encyclopedia article
  B. a letter written by a soldier to his brother during the war
  C. a biography of a prominent Union general during the war
  D. a novel set in northern Virginia that takes place during the war

Answer: B

Explanation: The soldier's letter to his brother is only source with firsthand account of events, making the letter a primary source.

QUESTION 26

Japan invaded India during World War II mainly because India

  A. was controlled by Japan's enemies.
  B. had once attacked Japan.
  C. had many natural resources.
  D. was a strategic location.

Answer: A

Explanation: Japan invaded India during World War II mainly because India was controlled by Japan's enemies. Japan wanted to attack the enemies.

QUESTION 27

The political situation in Africa today is heartening and at the same time disturbing. It is heartening to see so many new flags hoisted in place of the old; it is disturbing to see so many countries of varying sizes and at different levels of development, weak and, in some cases, almost helpless…The greatest contribution that Africa can make to the peace of the world is to avoid all the dangers inherent in disunity, by creating a political union which will also by its success, stand as an example to a divided world…The scant attention paid to African opposition to the French atomic tests in the Sahara, and the ignominious spectacle of the U.N. in the Congo quibbling about constitutional niceties while the Republic was tottering into anarchy, are evidence of the callous disregard of African Independence by the Great Powers. We have to prove that greatness is not to be measured in stockpiles of atom bombs.

The above is excerpt from Kwame Nkrumah, first President of Ghana. His ideas in the passage above are most representative of the ideology of

    A. liberation theology movement.
    B. anti-apartheid movement.
    C. Pan-Africanism.
    D. African American.

Answer: C

Explanation: Kwame Nkrumah is expressing the ideology of Pan-Africanism, which was a movement that aspired to encourage and strengthen bonds of solidarity between all people of African descent.

QUESTION 28

While conducting research on the United States politics of the late nineteenth century, a historian considers consulting the autobiography of a prominent politician who was alive in the late nineteenth century. Doing so is most likely to help the historian

    A. evaluate the long-term consequences of decisions made in the late nineteenth century.
    B. determine the exact sequence of events.
    C. obtain insight into contemporary values and beliefs.
    D. give perspective of individuals' feeling in the late nineteenth century.

Answer: C

Explanation: Since the historian is consulting the autobiography of a prominent politician who was alive in the late nineteenth century, the historian will get information on the values and beliefs of that time (contemporary).

QUESTION 29

Andrew Jackson's spoil system favored which group of individuals?

A. merchant
B. political advocates
C. peasants
D. common people

Answer: D

Explanation: Spoil system is a practice in political party. After winning an election, the winner gives government jobs to his or her voters/supporters as a reward for working toward victory, and as an encouragement to keep working for the party. This system favors the common people.

QUESTION 30

House Democrats overwhelmingly oppose the agreement, largely because of concerns of labor unions that the agreement would not adequately protect the rights of low-paid workers in Central America who would be competing more directly with U.S. workers. Many pro-trade, centrist Democrats are also declaring their opposition in order to voice their broader disagreement with Bush administration tax and domestic spending policies that they argue are not doing enough to equip the workforce to deal with a changing global economy.

The leaders of the Republican opposition to CAFTA are Reps. Walter B. Jones Jr. (N.C.) and Virgil H. Goode Jr. (Va.), both former Democrats. A number of Republicans who represent once-Democratic southern congressional districts heavily dependent on agricultural subsidies and tariff and quota protections for textiles also object to the treaty.

Under CAFTA, the United States would make permanent the temporary suspension of tariffs set by the Caribbean Basin Initiative. In return, the Dominican Republic, Honduras, Costa Rica, El Salvador, Guatemala and Nicaragua would reduce or eliminate tariffs on most imports, open state monopolies to foreign competition, and remove legal barriers to foreign investment.

Brown and Jones predicted the administration will begin offering special favors to wavering lawmakers. "They are going to open the bank for these guys," said Brown, citing past offers of bridges and other public works projects to win votes on controversial trade bills.

Washington Post, June 12, 2005
Based on the above reading from the Washington Post, the method likely to be effective for the White House to implement in passing the free trade legislation is

   A. executive order
   B. media
   C. pocket veto
   D. logrolling

Answer: D

Explanation: Logrolling is the practice of exchanging favors by reciprocal voting for each other's proposed legislation. The article states "the administration will begin offering special favors to wavering lawmakers".

QUESTION 31

> No one should be disquieted on account of his opinions, including his religious views, provided their manifestation does not disturb the public order established by law. - **French Declaration of the Rights of Man and Citizen (1789)**

The ideas and principles expressed in the quote above are most closely related to which of the following Enlightenment philosophers?

A. Voltaire
B. Jean-Jacques Rousseau
C. Baron de Montesquieu
D. Denis Diderot

Answer: A

Explanation: François-Marie Arouet, also known as Voltaire, was an outspoken advocate of civil liberties. He desired individuals to speak their minds without fear of consequences.

QUESTION 32

Which of the following appropriately describes a major check on the United States Supreme Court's power?

A. The Court has no authority in enforcing decisions.
B. The Court has no authority to modifying decisions.
C. The Court has no authority to overturning executive orders.
D. The Court can only hear cases that went through lower courts.

Answer: A

Explanation: The Supreme Court does not have the authority to enforce the decisions their make.

QUESTION 33

     I.   clearer separation of power between the branches of government
     II.   roles and responsibilities of public officials clearly outlined
     III.   greater cooperation between branches of government

Of the above, which of the following describes difference/differences between parliamentary democracies such as Great Britain and presidential democracies such as the United States?

    A. I only
    B. I and II
    C. I and III
    D. I, II and II

Answer: A

Explanation: There is a clear separation of power between the branches of government in presidential democracies in the United States than parliamentary democracies such as Great Britain.

QUESTION 34

> In all criminal prosecutions, the accused shall enjoy the right to a speedy and public trial, by an impartial jury of the state and district wherein the crime shall have been committed, which district shall have been previously ascertained by law, and to be informed of the nature and cause of the accusation; to be confronted with the witnesses against him; . . . and to have the assistance of counsel for his defense. – United States Constitution

In the quote from the United States Constitution, the meaning of which of the terms is best articulated?

    A. jurisdiction
    B. due process requirements
    C. equal protection
    D. witness protection

Answer: B

Explanation: To have the "right to a speedy and public trial" and to have "the assistance of counsel for his defense" are requirements of the due process system.

QUESTION 35

Which of the following events is most credited for surfacing the concept of natural rights?

    A. Enlightenment Period
    B. Industrial Revolution
    C. Age of Exploration
    D. Civil War

Answer: A

Explanation: Natural rights are those that cannot be repealed or restrained by human law. In other words, there are not dependent on the laws, customs, or government. Enlightenment Period was a time in history that is credited for the concept of natural rights. In this period, the words of Hugo Grotius, John Locke, and Samuel Pufendorf discussed the natural rights of individuals.

QUESTION 36

   1. Bill is referred to appropriate committee
   2. Names
   3. Voted on
   4. Signed by the president

The above process best reflects which of the following?

   A. pass a bill into a law in the House of Representatives
   B. pass a bill into a law in the Senate
   C. pass a bill into law under emergency conditions
   D. pass a bill into law in Congress

Answer: A

Explanation: The process described is to pass a bill into a law in the House of Representatives.

QUESTION 37

In the late nineteenth-century, America saw the expansion of the railroad system and the most significant result was

   A. increase jobs.
   B. spread of ideas.
   C. exchange of goods.
   D. more focus on technology.

Answer: C

Explanation: The railroad system allowed the movement of goods.

QUESTION 38

Which of the following constitutional provisions reflect the increasing intersectional tension within United States during 1850s?

- A. "No preference shall be given by any regulation of commerce or revenue to the ports of one state over those of another."
- B. "The President shall be Commander in Chief of the army and navy of the United States, and of the militia of the several states, when called into the actual service of the United States."
- C. "No state shall enter into any treaty, alliance, or confederation; grant letters of marque or reprisal; coin money; [or] emit bills of credit."
- D. "The Congress shall have power to dispose of and make all needful rules and regulations respecting the territory or other property belonging to the United States."

Answer: D

Explanation: There was increase tension regarding territory in the 1850s. Option D reflects the increasing intersectional tension within United States during 1850s. Option D is related to establishing rules and regulations that address the increasing intersectional tension.

QUESTION 39

Which of the following source is not useful in obtaining information about the Presidency of Richard Nixon?

    A. Richard Nixon's autobiography
    B. Speeches of Richard Nixon
    C. White House correspondence
    D. Richard Nixon's resignation letter

Answer: A

Explanation: Richard Nixon's autobiography is not going to be useful source as it does not exist. Richard Nixon did not write an autobiography.

QUESTION 40

The major reason for the extraordinary economic affluence of United States society approximately twenty years after World War II was because of which of the following?

    A. the United States industrial base was undamaged
    B. no major competition in the global market
    C. the devolution of the United States to become a superpower
    D. increase in wage control and exports and imports

Answer: B

Explanation: Economic distress was seen across the globe for many years after World War II. The impact of the war caused very little competition in the global market.

QUESTION 41

Bill of Rights is the first ten amendments to the United States Constitution. Which of the following principles of the United States Constitution best demonstrate the idea of the Bill of Rights?

    A. ability to overthrow government
    B. limited government
    C. rights of the people
    D. checks and balances

Answer: B

Explanation: The Bill of Rights was to prevent a tyrant government. The purpose was to limit the power of the government.

QUESTION 42

Which of the following geographic factors had the most significant influence on economic life in the early life of the people of Anatolia?

    A. the natural harbors along the Red Sea
    B. the aquatic resources of the Mediterranean Sea
    C. the resources of the Eastern Desert
    D. the annual flooding of the Nile River

Answer: B

Explanation: Anatolia is a vast plateau between the Black and the Mediterranean seas. The aquatic resources of the Mediterranean Sea were the significant influence on economic life in the early life of the people of Anatolia.

QUESTION 43

A recent college graduate is debating whether he should continue to obtain his graduate degree or accept a job offer for entry level position. Which of the economic concepts applies most directly to the decision the graduate is attempting to make?

    A. supply and demand
    B. cost of opportunity
    C. market demand
    D. productivity

Answer: B

Explanation: The student is debating to continue with education or start a new job. Both options involve cost, so the student is deciding the cost of the opportunities.

QUESTION 44

The Declaration of Independence states, "That whenever any form of government becomes destructive of these ends, it is the Right of the People to alter or abolish it." This statement describe the enlightened idea of a

    A. strong democracy.
    B. return to a society that has two central authority.
    C. social contract between the government and the people.
    D. right to overthrow the current government.

Answer: C

Explanation: The statement is a contract between the government and the people. The people have the right to alter or abolish the government if the government becomes destructive.

QUESTION 45

The following changes occurred in the United States in the 19ᵗʰ Century:

- improvements in agricultural production
- increases in immigration from Europe
- advancements in networks of railroad

The changes resulted in:

A. removal of large suburbs around cities
B. growth of urban areas
C. obtaining overseas territories
D. movement of people from the urban to rural areas

Answer: B

Explanation: The growth of urban areas caused improvements in agricultural production, increases in immigration from Europe, and advancements in networks of railroad.

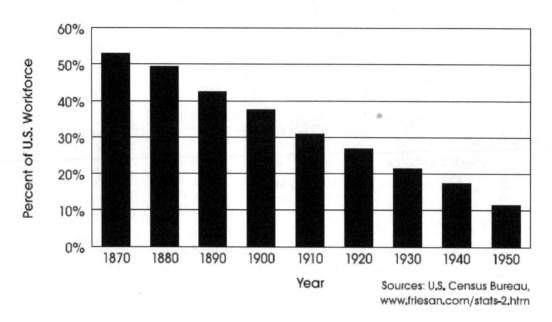

Percent of U.S. Workforce
Engaged in Farm Labor, 1870 – 1950

Sources: U.S. Census Bureau,
www.friesan.com/stats-2.htm

According to the graph above, the trend shown in the graph is associated with?

- A. decreased immigration
- B. increased urbanization
- C. reduced population growth
- D. advances in communication

Answer: B

Explanation: The decrease of workforce is linked to increase in urbanization. With the increase in urbanization, the processes became more efficient, and technologies replaced jobs. This caused reduced number in the workforce over the decades.

QUESTION 47

    I.   ability to sell stocks
    II.   limited liability for owners
    III.   improved ability to raise large sums of money

The items above are all benefits of which of the following?

    A.   monopolies
    B.   corporations
    C.   proprietorships
    D.   unionization

Answer: B

Explanation: Ability to sell stocks, limited liability for owners, and ability to raise large sums of money are benefits of corporations.

QUESTION 48

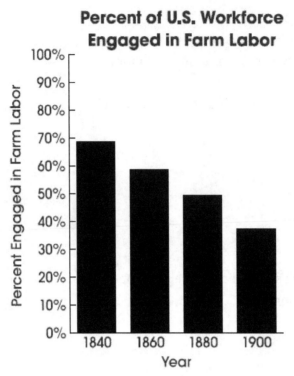

In the above graph, what effect of 19th century industrialization in the United States is shown in the above graph?

A. emigration from the United States
B. increased regulation of child labor
C. decreased demand for farm products
D. modernization of agriculture

Answer: D

Explanation: To answer the question, look at the title and the labels. The graph is about the percent of workforce engaged in farm labor. The percent of labor has declined over the decades. One possible reason for this is the modernization of agriculture. The modernization of agriculture resulted in less labor force needed.

QUESTION 49

The scientific revolution of the sixteenth and seventeenth centuries contributed most significantly in the thoughts fostered during the Enlightenment Period by which of the following?

A. The use of math to assist in understanding the relationships among diverse natural events.
B. The use of reason to devise laws to explain the physical world.
C. The use of science to assist in understanding the relationships among diverse natural events.
D. The use of math to devise the laws to explain the physical world.

Answer: B

Explanation: The scientific revolution of the sixteenth and seventeenth centuries contributed most significantly in the thoughts fostered during the Enlightenment Period by the use of reason to devise laws to explain the physical world.

QUESTION 50

Steam power was a critical invention in American History. During the earlier part of the nineteenth century, the increase usage of stem power directly resulted in all the following except:

A. revenue of factories
B. location of factories
C. productivity of factor
D. quality of goods produced

Answer: D

Explanation: The quality of good produced was not directly related to the steam power. All other options were the direct impact of the steam power.

QUESTION 51

In the late nineteenth century and early twentieth century, as a result of industrialization, progressive reformers wanted government regulation of business in order to

    A. stop companies from moving their factories to other countries.
    B. return competition by limiting the power of monopolies.
    C. control inflation and recession.
    D. provide money for public services.

Answer: B

Explanation: In the late nineteenth century and early twentieth century, as a result of industrialization, progressive reformers wanted government regulation of business in order to return competition by limiting the power of monopolies.

QUESTION 52

When a country's constitution mandates the branches of government to remain independent of other branches, it is adhering to the constitutional principle of

    A. checks and balances.
    B. separation of powers.
    C. popular sovereignty.
    D. bipartisanism.

Answer: B

Explanation: Separation of powers is the principle or system of vesting in separate branches the executive, legislative, and judicial powers of a government.

QUESTION 53

The United States Declaration of Independence and the French Declaration of the Rights of Man share the similarity by expressing the idea that governments must

A. provide equal rights to all men.
B. protect the right of people.
C. support religious beliefs.
D. provide equal education all individuals.

Answer: B

Explanation: Both documents expressed the idea that government must protect the right of the people.

QUESTION 54

In Southern states, sharecropping became a significant means of organizing agricultural production due to

A. signing of the Emancipation Proclamation.
B. the need to generate cash in the short term.
C. the refusal of Northern financiers to extend loans.
D. the long-term effect of Civil War.

Answer: D

Explanation: Sharecropping is when a landowner allows a tenant to use the land in return for a share of the crops produced on their portion of land. By the early 1870s, sharecropping had come to dominate agriculture across the cotton-planting South. Sharecropping became a significant means of organizing agricultural production due to the Civil War.

QUESTION 55

Which of the following is NOT a difference between the northern and southern sections of the United States between 1800 and 1860 prior to the Civil War?

   A. Larger population of European immigrants who settled in the northern states, resulting in greater population growth in the North as oppose to the South.
   B. The North had much more industrialized economy than the South.
   C. During the first half of the nineteenth century, factory production played an important role in the southern economy while agricultural played an important role in the northern economy.
   D. After the American Revolution, northern states gradually abolished slavery while human bondage remained a central feature of southern society.

Answer: C

Explanation: All the options are difference between the northern and southern sections of the United States between 1800 and 1860 prior to the Civil War except for Option C.

QUESTION 56

Which of the following is NOT an important relationship between the civil rights movement and the Civil War?

   A. Many African Americans and whites united to protest the racism and discrimination that existed in the United States.
   B. A more organized Civil Rights Movement came into being.
   C. During the 1950s and the early 1960s, Martin Luther King, Jr., emerged as an important leader of the Civil Rights Movement.
   D. Economic competition with the Soviet Union resulted in greater injustice in the United States among whites and blacks.

Answer: D

Explanation: All the options are relationship between the civil rights movement and the Civil War except for Option D. The Soviet Union had no impact on the injustice occurring in the United States.

QUESTION 57

Following World War II, the economic recovery of Japan primarily focused on

    A. developing an export economy.
    B. developing an import economy.
    C. rebuilding strong military.
    D. developing an agricultural economy.

Answer: A

Explanation: The key to recovery was the boom in exports of cars, electronics, and other products, which grew far more rapidly than imports.

QUESTION 58

In Latin American, all the following have limited development of transportation systems and communication system except?

    A. deserts
    B. rain forests
    C. river systems
    D. mountain regions

Answer: A

Explanation: Mountain ranges, rain forests, and river systems have limited development of transportation systems and communication systems.

QUESTION 59

I.   First Gulf War – President George H.W. Bush

II. World War I – President Woodrow Wilson

III. Vietnam War – President Gerald Ford

Of the above, which of the following accurately indicate the President during the war?

A. I, II, and III
B. I only
C. II only
D. I and II

Answer: A

Explanation: During the First Gulf War, George H.W. Bush was the President. During World War I, Woodrow Wilson was the President. During Vietnam War, five Presidents held the office; Dwight Eisenhower, John F. Kennedy, Lyndon Johnson, Richard Nixon and Gerald Ford.

QUESTION 60

Increase use of renewable fuels such as solar power or wind power could result in

    A. increase use of coal.
    B. increase dependence on nuclear generated power.
    C. less pollution in the environment.
    D. needing more foreign oil.

Answer: C

Explanation: Using renewable results in less dependence on oil, coal, nuclear power, and other resource because of reuse. Therefore, there is less pollution in the environment.

QUESTION 61

How do people survive in harsh environments such as the desert?

    A. They relocate to a better location.
    B. They adapt and make changes to their environment.
    C. They find food and shelter to meets needs.
    D. They establish civilization.

Answer: B

Explanation: The best choice and correct choice is to adapt and make changes to survive.

QUESTION 62

Which of the following was a main cause of the Cold War between the United States and the Soviet Union?

    A. desire to have greater influence on world economy
    B. desire to have greater influence on other nations
    C. desire to have greater control over oil prices
    D. desire to have greater control over export laws

Answer: B

Explanation: The need for countries to have greater influence on other nations was the main cause of the Cold War between the United States and the Soviet Union.

QUESTION 63

> One way of life is based upon the will of the people, and is distinguished by ... freedom from political oppression. The second way of life is based on the will of a minority forcibly imposed upon the will of the majority. It relies upon ...the suppression of personal freedoms.

In 1947, the above quote was delivered as part of which of the following speech?

- A. Monroe Doctrine
- B. Truman Doctrine
- C. New Deal Speech
- D. New Frontier

Answer: B

Explanation: Harry S. Truman was responsible for the Truman Doctrine. The quote came from the Truman Doctrine.

QUESTION 64

Which of the following is NOT a depiction of Hitler's Germany, Mussolini's Italy, and Stalin's Russia?

- A. All nations were totalitarian governments.
- B. Economy was governed by Marxist principles.
- C. Political opponents were tortured in each state.
- D. Desired to expand their borders.

Answer: B

Explanation: All options depict Hitler's Germany, Mussolini's Italy, and Stalin's Russia except for option B.

QUESTION 65

Which of the following was impacted the most due to the distribution of hydrocarbon resources in Africa, Latin America, and Middle East during the 20th century?

A. United States economy
B. world economy
C. international relations
D. price of oil

Answer: C

Explanation: The existence of hydrocarbon resources in Africa, Latin America, and Middle East impacted international relations. Countries need energy resources, so the relationships strengthen between counties.

QUESTION 66

In developed countries, around year 2000, majority of the people resided in towns and cities. Two hundred years prior, the population resided in rural areas. Which of the following most significantly contributed to the change?

A. increase in birth
B. modernization of transportation
C. industrialization of national economies
D. increase infrastructure

Answer: C

Explanation: In the United States, the change from towns and cities to rural areas was due to the industrialization of national economies.

QUESTION 67

What is a major difference between Buddhism and Hinduism?

   A. Buddhism refused the need for caste and rite to achieve nirvana.
   B. Buddhism was polytheistic and Hinduism was monotheistic.
   C. Buddhism did not accept the political world
   D. Hinduism focused on respect and not hurting individuals

Answer: A

Explanation: One of the differences is that Buddhism does not require the need for caste and rite to achieve nirvana.

QUESTION 68

   I.   rulers functioned as religious leader as well as heads of state
   II.   a class system based on merits and values
   III. a military based on only volunteer service

Of the above, which is/are common characteristic(s) of both Aztec and Incan civilizations?

   A. I only
   B. III only
   C. I and II
   D. II and III

Answer: A

Explanation: In both Aztec and Incan civilizations, rulers functioned as religious leader as well as heads of state.

QUESTION 69

Leaders of the Chinese Revolution broke most determinedly with Chinese past in their

A. emphasizes on materialism, science, and class conflict.
B. refusal to engage in other nations.
C. creation of a centralized government.
D. principal of communism.

Answer: A

Explanation: Leaders of the Chinese Revolution broke most determinedly with Chinese past related to materialism, science, and class conflict.

QUESTION 70

Which of the following is incorrectly defined?

	Type of Society	Definition
A	Hunting and Gathering Societies	Those peoples whose technology is de-signed to use primarily wild game and plant resources.
B	Horticultural Societies	People who depend the raising of livestock.
C	Agrarian Societies	Societies that depend mainly on plant cultivation, and that use draft animals and plows.
D	Commercial/Industrial Societies	Societies with a majority of the population engaged in trade and manufacturing.

Answer: B

Explanation: Horticultural societies that depend primarily on cultivated plants while lacking the use of draft animals and the plow.

QUESTION 71

Compared to river valley culture in Egypt and Mesopotamia, Chinese civilization

    A. had no reliable artifact left behind to study the civilization.
    B. probably did not rely on irrigation as other civilization did.
    C. likely developed after the Mesopotamia and Nile Valley civilization.
    D. likely developed at the same time as Mesopotamia and Nile Valley civilization.

Answer: C

Explanation: The only option that is true is Option C.

QUESTION 72

How did the Constitution address the quote: "He [King George III] has affected to render the Military independent of and superior to Civil power…?"

    A. the Constitution states that the president is the commander-in-chief of the military
    B. the Constitution prevents any revisions unless authorized by the president
    C. provided voting rights to all Americans
    D. gave citizens the right to bear arms

Answer: D

Explanation: The Constitution gives citizens the right to bear arms, which allows citizen to have protection over tyranny.

QUESTION 73

All the following are features of the Sumerian civilization except?

    A. an alphabet of 22 letters
    B. city-states
    C. ziggurats
    D. cuneiform

Answer: A

Explanation: Phoenician was responsible for the alphabet of 22 letters. Sumerian features include city-states, ziggurats, and cuneiform.

QUESTION 74

Which of the following is the best way a president can influence the opinions of the federal judiciary?

    A. increasing the number of justices on Supreme Court
    B. replacing Supreme Court justices at the beginning of the term
    C. appointing justices who share common political views
    D. keeping a personal relationship with the justices

Answer: C

Explanation: The President can appoint justices who share common political views to influence the opinions of the federal judiciary.

QUESTION 75

Which line on the table best matches a historical research question with the source of information that can used in providing information?

Line	Research Question	Source of Information
1	How did World War II impact the United States in the long term?	historical atlas
2	What roots did the principles of the Bill of Rights express?	biographical dictionary
3	How has the proportion of China population living in rural areas changed in the past decade?	almanac
4	How is the safety of our school system compared to several decades ago?	encyclopedia

    A. Line 1
    B. Line 2
    C. Line 3
    D. Line 4

Answer: C

Explanation: Almanac can include information on population statistics.

QUESTION 76

A librarian is doing a lesson on effective ways of teaching for group of middle school students. The topic for the week is primary and secondary sources. Librarian can inform the students that the most effective way to identify relevant secondary and primary sources is by

A. asking the teacher prior to making any conclusions.
B. consulting online research for confirmation purposes.
C. reviewing the citations and bibliography of texts related to the topics of research.
D. seeing what year the source was written and decide if it primary or secondary.

Answer: C

Explanation: Reviewing the citations and bibliography of the text will indicate if the sources used are secondary and primary.

QUESTION 77

A nation large in size with a heterogeneous population and conflicting needs is best suited with which type of government system?

A. unitary system
B. communistic system
C. federal system
D. state system

Answer: C

Explanation: A large nation with different types of individuals and different ideas and needs requires a federal system, which is a type of government where power is divided between a central authority and constituent political units.

QUESTION 78

I.   Department of Education
II.   Securities and Exchange Commission
III. Environmental Protection Agency

Of the above, which of the following policymaking powers is/are based on delegated legislative authority?

A. I only
B. I and II
C. I and III
D. II and III

Answer: D

Explanation: Securities and Exchange Commission and Environmental Protection Agency are policymaking powers based on delegated legislative authority.

QUESTION 79

	Building Art Exhibit		Expanding Library	
	Yes	No	Yes	No
James County	22,323	20,329	18,929	21,932

James County is looking to build an art exhibit or expand the library with tax payer funds. The above results were obtained in a recent special election on the issue. A history teacher wants to determine whether the residents of the country held strong opinions about these two issues. Clearly, the results above will support the researcher in the study, but what additional information will be most useful to the teacher?

    A. the age group of the individuals who voted
    B. any voters who would be bias in voting
    C. number of individuals who were eligible to vote
    D. the cost of building the exhibit and expanding the library

Answer: C

Explanation: Knowing the total number of eligible voters will inform the teacher if the results are giving a full picture of individuals' opinion.

QUESTION 80

Which of the following is NOT an enumerated power of Congress?

    A. declare war
    B. treaty ratification
    C. establish post offices
    D. all the above are powers of Congress

Answer: D

Explanation: Congress is involved in declaring war, ratifying treaty, and establishing post offices.

QUESTION 81

Which of the following powers allows Congress to indirectly impact foreign policy?

  A. approve and reject treaties
  B. approve or reject presidential appointments
  C. allocate federal funding
  D. regulate international commerce

Answer: C

Explanation: Federal funding is important aspect of government, and Congress can use that indirectly to influence foreign policy.

QUESTION 82

Social status is more likely to be determined by values not related to money in a pre-industrial society as oppose to which of the following society?

  A. industrial
  B. post industrial
  C. post Civil War
  D. post World War II

Answer: B

Explanation: Pre-industrial society determines social status by values while post-industrial society determines social status by money.

QUESTION 83

    I.   weakened the economics of major colonial power

    II.   increased prewar alliances major powers

    III.   demolished prewar alliances major powers

Which of the above way(s) did World War II impacted the decolonization in Africa and Asia?

    A. I only

    B. II only

    C. III only

    D. I and II

Answer: A

Explanation: After World War II, weakened economics of major colonial power impacted the decolonization in Africa and Asia.

QUESTION 84

Who was the first woman to contribute to women's right to vote?

    A. Eleanor Roosevelt

    B. Susan B. Anthony

    C. Elizabeth Cady Stanton

    D. Rosa Parks

Answer: C

Explanation: Elizabeth Cady Stanton was an early leader of the woman's rights movement. She held the Seneca Falls Convention in July 1848 where she took the lead in proposing that women be granted the right to vote.

QUESTION 85

I.   granting titles of nobility
II.   coining money
III.   establishing qualifications for voting

Under the Constitution, which is/are allowed to be undertaken by the states?

  A. I only
  B. III only
  C. I and II
  D. I and III

Answer: B

Explanation: States are allowed to establish qualifications for voting, such as the time, manner, and place of elections.

QUESTION 86

Level of Education	Average Salary
Doctoral Degree	$90,000
Master's Degree	$70,000
Bachelor's Degree	$60,000
Associate Degree	$50,000
Some College	$40,000
High School Graduate	$30,000
Some High School	$20,000

Which of the following conclusion can be made from the table?

  A. A doctoral degree will always make more than other degrees.
  B. Level of education is proportionally related to salary.
  C. Level of education is not proportionally related to salary.
  D. The quality of life for high school student is not going to be good as a college student.

Answer: B

Explanation: The higher the educational level achieved the higher the average salary. The change is proportional.

QUESTION 87

Which of the following is true about the Federal Reserve System?

    A. its seven Board members are appointed by the President of the United States
    B. its main policy-making body is called the CBO
    C. it insures checking accounts against bank failure
    D. it accepts deposits from individuals and makes loans for mortgages

Answer: A

Explanation: The President appoints the seven members of the Board of Governors of the Federal Reserve System.

QUESTION 88

    I.   decreased domestic investments
   II. increased private saving
  III. decreased foreign investments

Of the above, which is/are way(s) to finance a budget deficit?

    A. I only
    B. III only
    C. I and II
    D. I, II, and III

Answer: D

Explanation: Decreasing domestic investment, increasing private saving, and decreasing foreign investments are ways to finance a budget deficit.

QUESTION 89

John has a large sum of money to invest. He is very concerned with the risk, but not with the a large return. What is the best investment for him?

    A. checking account
    B. saving account
    C. real estate
    D. stock market

Answer: B

Explanation: Saving account has the least risk along with a lower return. Real estate and stock market have more risk. Typically, checking account is not used for investment purposes.

QUESTION 90

Which of the following is simple economic model illustrating the flow of goods and services?

    A. Circular flow model
    B. Loanable fund model
    C. Static model
    D. Dynamic model

Answer: A

Explanation: The circular flow of is a model of the economy in which the major exchanges are represented as flows of money, goods, and services.

Constructed Response Questions

Question 1

Read the information below; then complete the exercise that follows.

In American history, many significant documents have been written that has shaped our society today.

Bill of Rights, Declaration of Independence, Articles of Confederation, Common Sense

Using your knowledge of U.S. history, select two of the above documents and in your response:

- discuss two similarities of the documents
- discuss two differences of the documents
- discuss the long term impact of the documents

Response: Use email tutoring services to send constructed response to obtain detail feedback and scores.

Question 2

Read the two passages below; then complete the exercise that follows.

Alexander Hamilton, The Report on Manufactures (December 5, 1791)

The expediency of encouraging manufactures in the United States appears at this time to be pretty generally admitted. Not only the wealth, but the independence and security of a country, appear to be materially connected with the prosperity of manufactures. Every nation, with a view to those great objects, ought to endeavor to possess within itself all the essentials of national supply. These comprise the means of subsistence, habitation, clothing, and defense. A full view having now been taken of the inducements to the promotion of manufactures in the United States, it is proper to consider the means by which it may be effected. In countries where there is great private wealth, much may be effected by the voluntary contributions of patriotic individuals; but in a community situated like that of the United States, the public purse must apply the deficiency of private resource. In what can it be so useful, as in prompting and improving the efforts of industry?

Thomas Jefferson, Notes on the State of Virginia (1784)

Those who labour in the earth are the chosen people of God, if ever he had a chosen people, whose breasts he has made his peculiar deposit for substantial and genuine virtue. Corruption of morals in the mass of cultivators is a phenomenon of which no age nor nation has furnished an example. It is the mark set on those, who not looking up to heaven, to their own soil and industry, as does the husbandman, for their subsistence, depend for it [instead] on the casualties and caprice of customers. Dependence begets subservience and venality, suffocates the germ of virtue, and prepares fit tools for the designs of ambition.[G]enerally speaking, the proportion which the aggregate of the other classes of citizens bears in any state to that of its husbandmen, is the proportion of its unsound to its healthy parts, and is a good-enough barometer whereby to measure its degree of corruption. While we have land to labour then, let us never wish to see our citizens occupied at a work-bench, or twirling a distaff.

Using your knowledge of U.S. history, prepare a narrative response in which you:

-   explain the background historical context on how the two documents surfaced
-   compare and contrast the governmental actions Jefferson and Hamilton would likely support based on the excerpts

Response: Use email tutoring services to send constructed response to obtain detail feedback and scores.

Question 3

Analyze why some United States economists support and other United States economists resist on the idea of removing all restraints on the flow of capital and goods.

Response: Use email tutoring services to send constructed response to obtain detail feedback and scores.

PRAXIS® 5086 Social Studies: Content and Interpretation

By: Preparing Teachers In America™

CPSIA information can be obtained
at www.ICGtesting.com
Printed in the USA
LVHW061455240820
664070LV00014B/614